Cover illustration: Victor B.2R XL191 of the Wittering Wing (note the lion badge on the fin), at low level during the flypast for the RAF's 50th Anniversary Review by HM the Queen at Abingdon in 1968. (Wg. Cdr. A. Campbell)

1. Nine Vulcan B.2s of No. 83 Sqn. lined up at RAF Scampton in the early 1960s. Security on all V-bomber bases was tight, and RAF police dogs were frequently on unescorted patrol, especially in the more sensitive areas. The RAF Police sergeant is wearing the identity tag which was issued to all V-bomber base personnel; these tags were colour-coded with up to some half-a-dozen spots (which identified those areas of the station which the holder was cleared to enter), and also carried a photograph of the holder. The Vulcan nearest the camera is that of the Squadron Commander; it carries his Wing Commander's pennant aft of the No. 83 Sqn. crest on the fuselage. (British Aerospace)

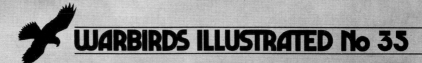

WARBIRDS ILLUSTRATED No 35

V BOMBERS

BOB DOWNEY

ARMS AND ARMOUR PRESS

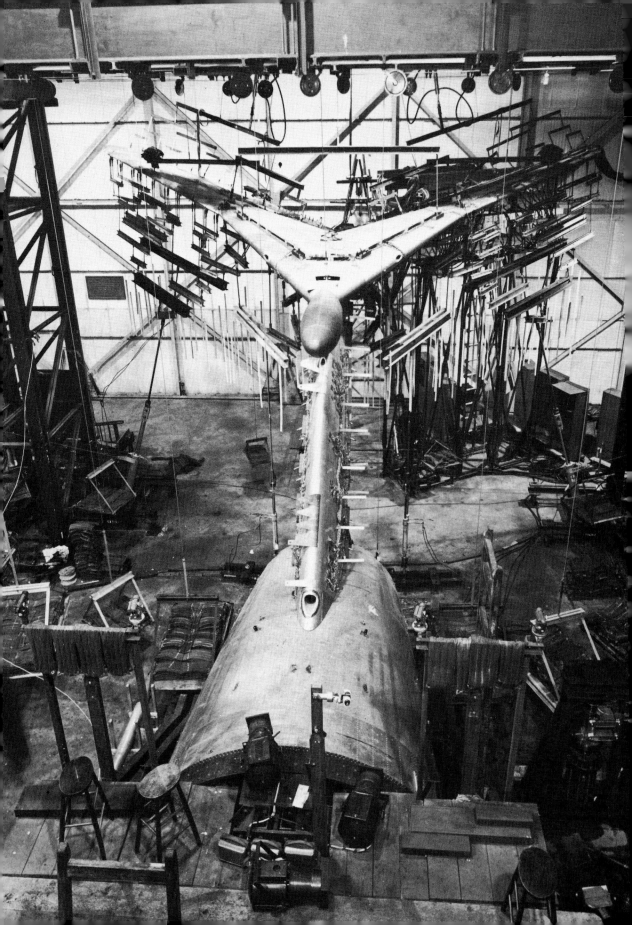

Introduction

blished in 1985 by Arms and Armour Press,
6 Hampstead High Street, London NW3 1QQ.

stributed in the United States by
erling Publishing Co. Inc., 2 Park Avenue,
w York, N.Y. 10016.

ritish Library Cataloguing in Publication Data:
owney, Bob
bombers. – (Warbirds illustrated; no. 35)
Victor (Jet planes)   2. Valiant (Bomber)
Vulcan (Bomber)
Title   II. Series
3.74'63'0941   UG242.B6
BN 0-85368-740-4

liting, design and artwork by Roger Chesneau.
ypesetting by Typesetters (Birmingham) Ltd.
inted in Italy by Tipolitografia G. Canale
C. S.p.A., Turin, in association with Keats
uropean Ltd.

Valiant, Victor, Vulcan – names which conjure up visions of strange and graceful white shapes wheeling in the skies over Farnborough or thundering in groups of four from airfields in the east of England. They are listed here in alphabetical order, for, like the nation which ordered, built and operated them, I cannot decide quite which of them was the best. What is clear, with the hindsight bestowed after nearly thirty years of consistent service in the Royal Air Force, is that all three V-bombers were truly multi-role aircraft, capable of adaptation either by initial design or by subsequent re-working. The Valiant came off the production lines in several versions, and the Victor and Vulcan were both adapted to roles which were not originally required of them. I have seen an Avro drawing of the Vulcan B.1 wing which was labelled 'B/PR/K Mk.1' and dated 1955, so obviously the company had outline plans for other roles which the RAF did not require until much later. I also recall one amusing incident in which an old Vulcan hand proceeded to describe Britain's latest aircraft type, the 'MRCV', and listed a host of roles from radar reconnaissance to ballistic and cruise missile carriage – the type being, of course, the Multi-Role Combat Vulcan. The point really is that these aircraft represented the finest products of the post-Second World War British aircraft industry, and for a time they were the equipment of the élite of the British armed forces.

This book does not concern itself with facts and figures, nor with such political questions as why certain weapon systems were taken from the V-bombers and why mid-life re-equipment programmes were not implemented; these are all areas which have been dealt with to some extent by other books. Neither does this selection of photographs claim to show all the variations in camouflage and markings carried by the V-bombers during their lengthy careers: even to show one aircraft of each type of each unit would take up more space than is available. What I have tried to do is to show some of the less publicized aspects of V-bomber operations, and to present photographs which may not be familiar to many people. Much of interest has had to be glossed over or even omitted, but I very much hope that the selection here meets with the approval of former V-Force personnel.

Very many people have given help in the production of this book, and it would be invidious to try to name all of them here. To those who have helped, and who are not mentioned elsewhere, my sincere thanks. However, three people deserve particular mention for their support of this project: Air Commodore R. M. Robson, OBE, Director of Public Relations (RAF) and a former commander of No. 27 (Vulcan B.2MRR) Squadron; Harry Holmes of British Aerospace Manchester Division; and Harry Fraser-Mitchell of BAe Kingston and the Handley Page Association. Photographs credited to British Aerospace are the copyright of British Aerospace plc; those acknowledged as RAF Official or Crown Copyright are RAF photographs, Crown Copyright Reserved. At the time of writing the Royal Air Force was operating a single Vulcan for display purposes based at RAF Marham under the title 'Vulcan Display Team'. No better tribute could be paid to the men who operated and maintained the V-bombers.

Bob Downey

◄2
. All three V-bombers were subjected to extensive tructural analyses and tests in an effort to predict their ltimate fatigue lives, although most of this work was irected at fatigue at high level, in which regime the ircraft were originally designed to perform. Here, a Victor tailplane assembly is being tested in a static tructural strength test rig designed to reproduce the ehaviour of the assembly during flight. (Handley Page Association)

▲3

▲4 ▼5

3. In its initial B.1 guise the Vickers Valiant was a very clean aeroplane, with very few external excrescences such as probes and aerials. This is WZ363, a B.1 serving with No. 38 Sqn. and photographed at RAF Valley in September 1957. (R. L. Ward)

4, 5. Early Valiants were left in natural metal finish, with the dielectric panels on the nose and fin being coated with the black protective sealant developed specially for this purpose; the rear part of the nose radome was painted grey. WZ403 was a B(K).1 serving with No. 207 Sqn. when photographed in 1957, whilst XD812 was photographed two months after delivery to the same unit in 1956. WZ403 carries the squadron crest on the fuselage nose.

6. By 1957 some Valiants were to be seen in the all-white paint finish, and one such was XD863 of No. 90 Sqn., photographed at RAF Honington in August of that year. The national markings are still in the original colours, and the serial is black; the 'XC' squadron badge on the fin is green with yellow letters.

7. The Valiant was the real pioneer of operational air-to-air refuelling techniques in the RAF, and here XD812, a B(K).1 of No. 214 Sqn., transfers fuel to WZ390, a B(PR)K.1 of the same unit. WZ390 had been serving with No. 214 Sqn. for two months when this photograph was taken in 1958; prior to this, the aircraft had been with Vickers for dry refuelling trials. (R. L. Ward)

▲8

▲9   ▼10

11▲

Wing-mounted auxiliary fuel tanks were an option increasingly [fit]ted to Valiants in service, as here on WZ377, a B(K).1 of No. [?] Sqn. seen at Honington in 1958. The aircraft has not been [eq]uipped with a refuelling probe, and so could only act as a tanker. [No]tice the silver-cloth individual wheel covers and intake blanking [pl]ate.
Even with wing tanks, the Valiant was a remarkably elegant aero[pl]ane, as demonstrated here by XD873, a B(K).1 of No. 207 Sqn., [fl]ying at the Open Day at Wethersfield in 1960. Notice the unit [ba]dge on the fin, the squadron crest on the nose, and the small Wing [Co]mmander's pennant beside the crest. The long flight-refuelling [pr]obe is fitted, and the photograph shows the pronounced nose-down [gr]ound attitude of the aircraft.
[?]. No. 214 Sqn. was the RAF's premier flight-refuelling squadron,

and was equipped with the Valiant B(K).1 for a time. This aircraft, XD870, carries the Flight Refuelling Ltd. emblem (similar to BOAC's 'Speedbird' symbol) with the diving nightjar of the squadron's original badge incorporated. Note the unit crest beneath the cockpit.
11. XD872, a Valiant B(K).1 of No. 90 Sqn., shows clearly the absence of underwing serials and pale markings which were a feature of later all-white aircraft. The aeroplane is in the low-speed flight condition, and shows the extensive flap area and the massive undercarriage structure.
12. XD857 was a Valiant which served only with one unit, No. 49 Sqn. It is seen here at Luqa, Malta, in August 1962, white overall and with pink/pale blue national markings and pale blue serials.

12▼

▲13

▲14   ▼15

13, 14, 15. No. 543 Sqn. was equipped with Valiant B(PR)K.1s – truly multi-role aircraft! – and was engaged in strategic reconnaissance duties. The majority of its aircraft retained the white finish, but variations in the application of its distinctive unit badge were common. WZ382 (photograph 13) carries the badge on the wing tanks only, while WZ394 (14) has it on both fin and tanks. WZ391 (15) was photographed in September 1964, still in white finish and carrying a squadron crest (and, like WZ382, a kangaroo 'zap') on the nose in addition to unit badges on fin and tanks.

16. The Bomber Command Development Unit was a little-publicized organization, based at RAF Finningley and responsible for the development of tactics, including electronic warfare procedures, for the V-Force. WZ400 was completed as a Valiant B(K).1 and is seen here resplendent with the unit's badge on the fin, above the flash, at the Finningley Battle of Britain Display in September 1962.

17, 18. A number of Valiants were involved in cold-weather trials work, and some received special paint schemes for this purpose. These Valiant B(K)PR.1s of No. 543 Sqn., WZ380 and WZ399, were photographed at RAF Wyton in August 1958, resplendent with red upper fins and with red areas on the wings. Notice the absence of any unit badges and of repeated serials on the nose-wheel doors.

19. No. 199 Sqn. was one of the more interesting Valiant units, with first its 'C' Flight and then, after September 1957, the whole squadron equipped with B.1s specially modified for the electronic countermeasures role. The aircraft were not externally distinguishable from other marks (as shown here by the first aircraft so equipped to be delivered to the unit, WP213), the main change being the replacement of the nose radar unit with a new turbo-alternator to power active jamming equipment.

16 ▲

17 ▲

18 ▲   19 ▼

11

▲20

20, 21. When No. 199 Sqn. moved from Honington to Finningley at the end of 1958 it changed 'plates' and became No. 18 Sqn., though still flew in the ECM role. WZ372 and WP211 were two of these aircraft. The latter is seen at the Finningley 'At Home' day in September 1960, and WZ372 was photographed at its home base a year later. WZ372 shows some external evidence of its specialized role, with a small dark panel on the tailcone side and an unusual item of equipment, purpose not known, on the upper wing root.

22, 23. A Valiant was involved in trials conducted by the Martin-Baker company to answer the need for rear-crew ejection seats, and Mr. W. T. 'Doddy' Hay carried out a number of ejections from an experimental installation mounted in Valiant B.1 WP199 in 1960.

▼21

Martin-Baker also designed a three-ejection seat system for rear cre in Vulcans, and the test rig for this is shown in photograph 23. The installation involved a hatch above the centre seat, which was jettisoned in a controlled sequence before the centre seat left the aircraft. The two side seats were then tilted towards the aperture an ejected, thus completing the automatic sequence and permitting the operation of the pilots' seats. Despite the elegance of the solution, there was never sufficient pressure from the right quarters to carry a retrofit programme through, although if it had been envisaged in 1959 that Vulcans would still be in front-line service in 1982, authority would doubtless have been given. (Martin-Baker Aircraft Co.)

22▲   23▼

▲24

▲25 ▼26

25, 26. The Vickers
▲eld at Hurn was the
▲or base for modifi-
▲on and development
▲k with the Valiant,
▲these three aircraft
▲e photographed there
▲ing 1961. B.1 WP208
▲ undergoing a minor
▲ection, WZ370 was
▲ng held there prior to
▲very in May 1961 to
▲ Radar Research
▲ablishment,
▲shore, and WZ384
▲ undergoing modifi-
▲on work while
▲ving with No. 148
▲.

▲ Despite its large size,
▲ Valiant was by no
▲ans a sedate aircraft,
▲emonstrated here by
▲. Lt. Tony Banfield at
▲ton in 1962. The air-
▲me was well-suited to
▲-level manoeuvring,
▲ough ultimately the
▲ucture itself could not
▲e much of this sort of
▲ng and the fatigue
▲blems encountered
▲e the Valiant force
▲nt low-level opera-
▲nally caused the
▲apping of nearly every
▲craft. WZ391 was a
▲PR).1 serving with
▲. 543 Sqn. at Wyton.
▲. L. Ward)

, 29. With the decision
▲ operate the V-force in
▲ low-level attack role
▲ring 1964, a number of
▲liants were repainted
▲an upper surface
▲mouflage scheme of
▲dium Sea Grey and
▲rk Green. This change
▲ncided with the intro-
▲ction of centralized
▲vicing, which meant
▲t individual aircraft
▲ longer carried
▲uadron identifications.
▲D821 (photograph 28)
▲s a B(K).1 of No. 232
▲perational Conversion
▲nit (OCU), while
▲Z395 (29), also a
▲K).1, was with the
▲arham Wing and is
▲en here at Luqa in
▲ugust 1964.

27▲

28▲   29▼

15

▲30

▲31　▼32

16

, 31. Two interesting photographs, taken at Marham in 1965, ortly after all four Valiants were struck off charge on 5 March of at year. The aircraft were posed for these official 'last photographs' the ORP at the end of Runway 24. XD829, in the foreground, was (K).1, WZ393 a B(PR)K.1 and XD822 another B(K).1; the urth aircraft is also an XD-series airframe, and was thus a B(K).1. ote the slight variations in the camouflage schemes and the white-inted tailcones of the first, second and fourth aircraft. (Crown pyright via K. Austin)

. Only one Valiant out of some 107 produced was earmarked for eservation after the sudden withdrawal of the type early in 1965. ppropriately enough, this was a historic airframe, XD818 – the craft from which Britain's first thermonuclear bomb was dropped in Operation 'Grapple' in May 1957. The aircraft, a B(K).1, was preserved at RAF Marham, where it is seen in this photograph before transfer to the Bomber Command Museum at Hendon. It is now displayed in the all-white scheme. (Author)

33, 34. Two views of Handley Page Victor B.1 XA930 prior to delivery to the RAF. Illustration 33 reveals details of the mounting of the flight-refuelling probe above the cockpit, and note also the white lines through the upper roundels; photo 34 shows the underwing fuel tanks to advantage and also the original chaff dispenser ports beneath the nose, immediately in front of the nosewheel bay. Distinct edges to areas of staining on the underside are evident, particularly beneath the inner wings. (Handley Page Association)

▲35

35. Another view of XA930, this time at the 1958 SBAC Show at Farnborough. In this and the previous two photographs three black rectangles are visible on the nose, just below the rear crew porthole; these were for photographic reference. National markings are carried in dark colours on this aircraft, which served with No. 15 Sqn. before being converted to K.1A standard. (R. L. Ward)

36. XA932, a Victor B.1 of No. 10 Sqn., at Mildenhall in June 1961. The aircraft, which is white overall, has national markings in dark colours and its serial in black (with a smaller version on the nose-wheel doors), and carries the squadron's winged arrow badge in red, gold and black on the fin and its crest on both sides of the nose beneath the canopy. A point of interest is that the fin bullet has a blue/red/blue stripe painted around it.

37, 38, 39. Three Victor B.1s of No. 232 OCU reveal subtle differences in what appear at first sight to be 'standard' markings. XA933 has national insignia in dark colours and serial in black (with smaller version painted on both nosewheel doors); XA931 carries the letter 'A' on the fin above the fin flash – a feature of the Victor OCU aircraft – and, again, has the serial repeated on the nosewheel doors (but positioned further forward); and XA925, photographed on the same day as '931, carries the letter 'A' as well, but has national markings, serial and code letter in pale colours, pale blue being used for the code letter and the serial. The last machine does not have the serial repeated on the nosewheel doors.

▼36

▲ 40

▲ 41

▲ 42   ▼ 43

40. By July 1960 most No. 57 Sqn. Victor B.1 had been adorned with small squadron badge – Phoenix rising from burning logs – on the fin. This aircraft also carrie Squadron Leader's pennant beneath the cockpit canopy. Nation markings are still in dar colours, and the serial, carried only on the fuselage, is black. Notic the slight darkening of the fairing covering the nose-mounted radar (known as the NBS scanner – Navigation an Bombing System) due t the different materials used in its construction.

41. Victor B.1 XH591 o No. 15 Sqn., photographed in September 1960, carries the distinctive squadron badge on the fin above the flash and the squadron crest on the nose, immediately beneath the ejection sea warning triangle. A feature of No. 15 Sqn. B.1s was the repetition o the aircraft serial on bot nosewheel doors. Notic the small open hatch on the fuselage beneath the air intakes, with ground power supplies connected into it. The leading edge slats are extended.

42. Victor B.1 XH614 of No. 57 Sqn., summer 1959. The aircraft is devoid of any markings except the serial and the national insignia, which are applied in the norma shades. The aircraft was later converted to B.1A, and subsequently to K.1A, standard.

43. All-white operationa aircraft quickly became weathered from normal usage, although the public usually saw specially cleaned machines at air shows. This No. 10 Sqn. Victor B.1 exhibits much evidence of usage, especially around the latches of the underfuselage access panels where dirt and oil have not been washed away by the airflow. The aircraft was photographed at Cottesmore in September 1963.

44. A Victor B.1A of No. 15 Sqn. in a Cottesmore hangar in late 1961. The aircraft had returned early from a night sortie with no apparent external damage apart from scorch marks on the No. 3 engine doors. In fact the crew had narrowly missed a major catastrophe, as a hot-air bleed pipe from the engine had severed and had been blasting engine-temperature air through the bomb bay wall and against hydraulic components and electrical cables, stripping all the insulation of a section of loom in the wing root and resulting in a solid block of 150 wires. The Handley Page working party also found that the rubber bag of No. 1 right-hand fuel tank had melted, so that the entire aircraft was akin to a flying bomb for the last hour of the sortie. XH618 was later converted to K.1A standard and met a tragic end, colliding with a Buccaneer over the North Sea in the 1970s. (Stan Perry)

45. By early 1964 some of the No. 139 Sqn. Victor B.2s had been equipped with the new electronic countermeasures (ECM) suite, as shown here by the series of faired antennae around the tailcone of XL158. This aircraft was a Blue Steel-equipped B.2R, and a missile is here in the process of being installed on the aircraft at RAF Wittering.

46. Most all-white Victor B.2s of No. 100 Sqn. had the unit badge, a white skull and crossbones on a pale red disc, on the fin, although some carried a plain blue disc. XM718 reveals the subtle differences in the colour-ing of the underfuselage panels: that beneath the serial number is for the Doppler radar, and the main radar dielectric panel beneath the cockpit is also clear.

44 ▲

45 ▲   46 ▼

21

▲48

▲49 ▼50

47. (Previous spread) The Handley Page production shed at Radlett, showing final assembly of Victors. Interestingly, most aircraft are B.1s, although the centre aircraft (with tailplane installed) is a B.. The front three aircraft are almost complete, and fitting-ou is in progress, whilst technician are working inside the air intakes and radar bay of the B.2 (Handley Page Association)

48. This Victor B.2 of No. 139 Sqn., seen in September 1962, i finished in the standard anti-flash scheme of overall white with pale red/blue national markings. Notice the open access door to the storage compartment in the rear fuse-lage aft of the roundel, and the absence of tailcone ECM aerials at this time.

49. XA918 was the prototype Victor tanker, and first flew in August 1964 equipped with a Flight Refuelling FR.17 Hose Drum Unit in the flash-bomb bay and two FR.20B HDUs in underwing pods, plus additiona fuel tankage in the bomb bay. The aircraft was used exten-sively by A&AEE Boscombe Down for trials, and is seen here on one of these, clearing the Vulcan B.2 for refuelling from the centre hose, which is fully extended. Note the alignment marks painted beneath each wing, next to the pods. The Vulcan is a late airframe with 300-Series engines.

50. A number of Victor B.1 air-frames were returned to Handley Page's Radlett facility during 1964 for conversion into K.1/1A tankers, and XA937 is seen here outside the main building at Radlett. The aircraft had previously served with No. 10 Sqn., whose badge is still on the fin.

51. In the summer of 1968, RAF Strike Command was formed by amalgamating the former Fighter and Bomber Com-mands, and a ceremony was held at Scampton during which Bomber Command formally stood down. Valiant B(K).1 XD816 was specially flown in from Wisley for this event, still resplendent in its white finish and No. 214 Sqn. badge. This was the last Valiant to fly, being returned to storage at Wisley after its visit to Scampton. (J. C. Pickup)

52. Valiant B(K).1 XD824 was serving with No. 49 Sqn. when it was photographed at Luqa, Malta, in 1964. (Wg. Cdr. A. Campbell)

51▲   52▼

▲53   ▼54

55▲

56▲

. XA928 was a Victor B.1 of No. 10 Sqn., and is shown here at
ose Bay in 1959. Notice the distinctive blue/red/blue stripes
rried on the fin bullet fairings of this unit's aircraft at this time.
e bomb bay doors are open for servicing. (Carlos Price)
. The reconnaissance package of the Victor SR.2 was much neater
an that of the Valiant, being enclosed in modular bomb bay crates,
shown here by XH572 of No. 543 Sqn. At the front of the bomb
y is a photoflash crate; in the centre is the main crate containing
me fourteen cameras. (R. L. Ward)
. Victor K.2 XL164 of No. 57 Sqn., RAF Marham, photographed

from the roof of one of the hangars at Goose Bay in May 1980. Goose
Bay was the normal staging airfield in Canada for V-Force aircraft
deployments to North America. (Nigel Jones)
56. All three V-bombers, at Goose Bay in 1959. Vulcan B.1 XA911
is from No. 83 Sqn. at RAF Waddington, the Victor is a B.1 of No.
10 Sqn. and the Valiant, XD873, is a B(K).1 of No. 207 Sqn.
(Carlos Price)
57. Vulcans and ECM support Valiants at Goose Bay on a special
exercise in the late 1950s. Note the support Hastings on the left of the
line-up. (Carlos Price)

57▼

▲58

58. XH498 of No. 617 Sqn. staged through Goose Bay en route to Nellis AFB for the 1959 World Congress of Flight, and is seen here taxying past one of the hangars at Goose. (Carlos Price)

59. A head-on view of a Vulcan B.2 at an air display at Finningley in the early 1960s. The ground-handling equipment is painted blue,

and note the interesting, tarpaulin-draped bomb-trolley on the right (D. Ashley)

60. XL360, a Vulcan B.2A of the Scampton Wing, photographed in 1968 at its home base and carrying a Blue Steel missile. Note the glossy paint finish. (J. C. Pickup)

▼59

▼60

. A Victor B(PR).1 of the Radar Reconnaissance Flight, RAF
yton, in 1961. This unit was part of the Central Signals Establish-
ent, and was equipped with a total of four specially modified Victor
.1s. No details of the equipment carried by these aircraft are
ailable, except that one of the installations was codenamed 'Yellow
ster'. The only external markings visible on XA923 are small green
ghtning flashes on each side of the nose, and from a distance the
rcraft is visually indistinguishable from the standard B.1.
R. L. Ward)

. A Victor B.2R of No. 139 (Jamaica) Sqn. shortly after the unit
came operational with the type and with the Blue Steel stand-off
omb. XL512 is finished overall in white, high-reflectivity paint,
ith pale blue and pink roundels and fin flash. The serial is pale blue,
id the squadron badge appears to be in pale colours. The aircraft is
quipped with the full Retrofit ECM suite, including tail-warning

radar, active jammers and extra chaff dispensers. The Blue Steel
is also white overall, and note that the ventral fin of the missile
is folded. (Crown Copyright via Gp. Capt. M. J. Milligan)
63. A Victor B.1A of No. 15 Sqn., photographed in September 1964,
reveals the pattern of the camouflage scheme of Medium Sea Grey
and Dark Green which was applied over the original white finish
when the V-Force adopted low-level attack procedures. The undersides were kept white, the theory being that they would be most likely
to be presented to a thermonuclear blast when the aircraft performed
its post-delivery escape manoeuvre. Victor B.1A aircraft were easily
recognizable in side profile by the modified tailcone, housing a tail-
warning radar scanner, and by the ventral fairing aft of the bomb
doors and beneath the roundel. With the change to camouflage,
national markings were applied in standard colours.

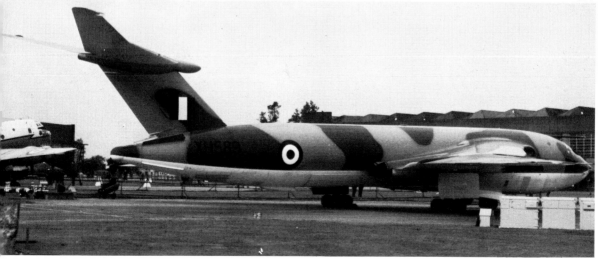

64. A factory-fresh Victor B.2, XL513, resplendent in its new upper surface camouflage scheme, reveals some of the anomalies in markings which were apparent when the V-Force went low-level. Whilst the fin flash is in standard dark colours, the fuselage roundel remains in the original pale blue/pink and the serial pale blue. Notice also the fine detail of the tailcone ECM antennae installations, with the darker dielectric portion of the lower one being particularly clear against the white of its fairing.

▲65

65. XM715 was a standard Victor B.2, and this photograph shows well the uppersurface camouflage pattern which was applied, with minor variations, to the Victor force during 1963–64. Note that a roundel is carried above the port wing only. (Crown Copyright)

66. Victor K.1 tankers of No. 214 Sqn. seen on the 29 end of Runway 11/29 at RAF Marham in the summer of 1969; prior to the closure of this runway, the aircraft were located in conventional dispersals. No. 214 was still the premier tanker squadron at the time, and still carried the badge using the 'Speedbird' symbol, two of latter depicted linked by a hose. (K. L. Austin)

67. Three Victor K.1As on the ramp at RAF Akrotiri in 1969. XH614 and XH645 (foreground) are from No. 55 Sqn., whilst the

third aircraft is from No. 214 Sqn. The aircraft are marked and camouflaged in the standard way, with a roundel on the port upper wing only. The Vulcans on the right are from the NEAF Bomber Wing, comprising Nos. 9 and 35 Sqns., the aircraft to the left (possibly XJ784) carrying blue/red roundels and fin flash. (Crown Copyright via Gp. Capt. M. J. Milligan)

68. A Victor B.1A of the Tanker Training Flight photographed in the summer of 1969. The TTF logo was carried on both sides of the fin immediately above the fin flash, the letters being painted red with white borders. The flight was renamed No. 232 OCU in 1970, and provided role conversion for crews posted to the tanker squadrons. Notice that wing pods are not fitted. (K. L. Austin)

▼66

67▲   68▼

▲69

69. The Victor B.2R was in many ways a less satisfactory Blue Steel carrier than the Vulcan, owing mainly to its very limited ground clearance, which made servicing of the missile/aircraft combination difficult; XL233 of the Wittering Wing, photographed in 1964, shows this problem clearly. The aircraft is painted in the then-new uppersurface camouflage of gloss Dark Green and Medium Sea Grey, with white undersides. National markings are in standard colours, and the serial is black. No unit badges are carried.

70. Victor B.2R XL190 of the Wittering Wing, photographed in September 1964. Notice in particular the paint demarcation around the undersides of the air intakes, and the subtle variations in shade under the nose section. This aircraft has chaff dispensers fitted in the wing trailing-edge Whitcomb bodies, as well as the full ECM suite of the MK.2 V-bombers.

▼70

By mid-1964 the process of camouflaging the V-Force was well in [ha]nd, and Victor B.2R XH671 of the Wittering Wing had been [p]ainted by September of that year, when it was photographed at [R]AF Luqa, in Malta. The aircraft is Blue Steel-equipped but is not [car]rying a missile: notice the large fairing at the front of the bomb bay [for] the Blue Steel's avionics heat-exhanger. The typical array of air [tro]lleys and ground power units surrounding the aircraft and the [prot]ective covers over all wheels are also of interest.

73. Not much was ever said about the exact nature of the ECM [in]stallation in the V-bombers, except that Vulcan and Victor Mk. 2 [air]craft were to receive the same equipment, which has subsequently [be]en described as 'noise jammers operating on certain radar [fr]equencies'. The installation on the Vulcan is noted elsewhere, but

that of the Victor has always been described as consisting of various antenna fairings around the tailcone. These two photographs, however, lead to different conclusions, for XL512, a B.2R of the Wittering Wing (photograph 72; note yellow lion on fin) has no tailcone bumps but does have a large blade aerial and three small dome aerials beneath the nose aft of the radar scanner fairing, while another B.2R, XL162 (photograph 73), has both under-nose and tailcone installations. The under-nose installations match exactly the aerial fit on the flat plate beneath the starboard jetpipes of the Vulcan B.2, although the large blade was usually fitted in place of one of the smaller dome aerials in the case of the Vulcan. (Handley Page Association/British Aerospace)

72▼

73▼

▲74 ▼75

76▲

. The Victor SR.2, which saw service with No. 543 Sqn., was
uipped with a formidable array of cameras and photoflash bombs
r night photography. Here a camera crate, which fitted into the
mb bay as a complete unit, is loaded with film magazines
mediately prior to a sortie; the cameras point downwards at
rious angles for pure vertical or oblique photography. Notice the
:ticework deflector visible at the front of the bomb bay opening,
d the massive towing arm attached to XL161's nosewheel. The
uadron crest appears on the large badge beneath the cockpit
ndows. (Crown Copyright)

. For a number of years the Victor K.2 tanker force operated with
e aircraft painted in a standard colour scheme of Dark Green and
edium Sea Grey on the uppersurfaces and white undersides. The
rcraft operated for the most part as a tactical tanker force in support
Air Defence of the United Kingdom fighter aircraft. Training for
rcrews was provided by No. 232 OCU at RAF Marham, and for a
hile this unit had its markings on XL232, seen here at Marham in
980. The machine exhibits the heavy weathering of a hard-working
OCU aircraft, and the white-painted Mk. 20 refuelling pods beneath
the wings carry dayglo red stripes. (Author)

76, 77. In the wake of the Falklands War of 1982, a number of
changes in both equipment and camouflage were made to the Victor
K.2 tanker force, and the camouflage changes in particular resulted
in a few oddities. The K.2 shown in photograph 76, XL191 of No. 55
Sqn., carries standard grey/green camouflage, but the starboard
auxiliary fuel tank is finished in the new Hemp and Light Aircraft
Grey scheme, and has obviously come from another aircraft. In
photograph 77, XH673, No. 57 Sqn., has the new Hemp uppersurfaces and Light Aircraft Grey undersides, with toned-down
markings. The new scheme includes the underwing Mk. 20
refuelling pods, and national markings are much smaller and painted
in pale colours. The aircraft carries the unit's Phoenix badge in
standard red/blue on the fin, with the unit's number in roman
numerals beneath. Both aircraft were seen at RAF Marham in
September 1984, by which time they had been equipped with new
electronics mounted at both ends of the fin bullet fairing. (Author)

77▼

▲78

78. VX777 was the second prototype Avro Vulcan, powered by four Olympus 102 engines; it is seen here on take-off from Woodford. At this stage in its career, '777 had been fitted with the B.2 type wing. Points to note are that the aircraft never had the characteristic black-coated nose radome or fin cap, and that it carries the serial beneath both wings. The small projection on the rear fuselage is a retractable tail bumper. (British Aerospace)

79. VX777 was flown to RAE Farnborough in April 1960 for ground armament tests and was struck off charge there in October 1962. The aircraft is seen here at Farnborough in September 1962, and already has lost its rudder and looks fairly heavily weathered. The national markings were applied in the normal colours. Notice that, since being fitted with the B.2 wing, the aircraft has dual pitot tubes mounted on the fuselage nose, and note also that the nose cone differ from that on production machines, the prototypes not being fitted with radar. (R. L. Ward)

▼79

9. The first Vulcan B.1s in RAF service were left in natural metal finish, except for the fin cap and forward part of the radome, which had a special black protective coating, and the rear part of the nose dome, which was grey. XA896 was serving with No. 230 OCU when photographed in 1958; this aircraft was later allocated to an engine test-bed role in connection with the P.1154 VTOL fighter project, and was scrapped when that programme was cancelled.

81. By 1958 Vulcans were in service with squadrons in all-white finishes, as shown here by XH481, a B.1 serving with No. 101 Sqn. In a reversal of later practice, the aircraft carries the squadron crest on the fin and the badge aft of the fuselage roundel. Notice the pronounced nose-up attitude of the B.1 and the absence of any upper fuselage blade aerials on this particular aircraft.

81▼

82. XH504 was delivered to No. 230 OCU in 1958 as a standard
Vulcan B.1, in which form it is seen here with the OCU badge on the
fuselage and a large City of Lincoln shield on the fin. Notice the
distinctive auxiliary air scoop on the fuselage just beneath the intake
splitter plate, the short jetpipes, and details of the wing upper
surfaces. XH504 was later converted to B.1A standard and served
with No. 101 Sqn. and the Waddington Wing prior to retirement at
Cottesmore early in 1968. (British Aerospace)

▲83　▼84

85 ▲

86 ▲

83, 84. When equipped with the Vulcan B.1 – such as XH499 (photograph 83) – No. 617 Sqn. carried only the squadron crest on the fuselage sides, the size of which equalled the diameter of the red portion of the fuselage roundel. The crest of the B.1A-equipped No. 50 Sqn., seen in photograph 84 on XH475, was of much smaller proportions, and the national markings were also in pale colours. The fin badge is the City of Lincoln shield, carried by all Waddington-based Vulcans. Note the addition of upper and lower UHF blade aerials on the B.1A, the lower being fitted to the visual bombing blister and the upper to the fuselage in front of the larger VHF blade aerial carried by all marks of Vulcan. Early UHF blade aerials were swept back, as shown here.

85, 86, 87. In October 1959 four Vulcan B.1s of No. 617 Sqn. left Scampton on a navigational exercise combined with a goodwill visit to New Zealand. During their stay in that country, XH498 was to fly in to Wellington Airport in order to form part of the static aircraft display at the official opening of the airport. Unfortunately, it proved impossible for the pilot to land on the relatively short runway, and he overshot twice. On the third attempt the Vulcan's main undercarriage struck the runway's undershoot area, resulting in damage to the port leg. The aircraft was kept under control by Sqn. Ldr. Tony Smailes, who flew it to RNZAF Ohakea, where he executed a superb forced landing. In photograph 85, '498 has come to rest; John Knight is just leaving the cockpit while Wally Huggett, another crew member, is on the wing. Note that, although the rear crew did not bale out, the canopy was jettisoned in accordance with standard procedures for forced landings. Photograph 86 shows the damaged port main undercarriage of XH498; note the fairly minimal damage to the rest of the airframe. The aircraft remained at Ohakea for many months, but was subsequently returned to service. In photograph 87, XH502, another of the four aircraft in the deployment, overflies the stricken XH498 at Ohakea. (Wg. Cdr. Bryn Lewis)

87 ▼

▲88

88. A view of XH498 later in its career, after repairs had been carried out and its conversion to B.1A standard completed. Now serving with the Waddington Wing, the aircraft is camouflaged on the upper surfaces but has recently had the refuelling probe removed and a white blanking plate fitted in its place. (Ray Leach)

89. In 1960 a Vulcan B.1 of No. 101 Sqn., captained by Flt. Lt. Eric Denham, made a 'Lone Ranger' sortie to Nairobi, Kenya. These single-aircraft trips were as much a test of maintenance as of navigation, since the crews were totally responsible for the aircraft, which was usually equipped with a bomb bay travel pannier containing such items as spare tyres, parts, brake parachutes and the like. This particular sortie was to gain some publicity, as a correspondent was aboard and a report subsequently appeared in *The Times*; it also began dramatically when two engines flamed-out in quick succession. Following a successful relight of one engine, Flt.

Lt. Denham returned to base, and the crew took over XA912, which completed the round trip without problems. The photograph shows XA912 passing over the cone of Mount Kilimanjaro. (Via Eric Denham)

90. One of the features of Vulcan operations throughout the 1970s and early 1980s was participation in the annual Strategic Air Command 'Giant Voice' bombing competition. XM653, seen here at Barksdale AFB in October 1974, carries the No. 1 Group RAF panther's head badge on the fuselage and a large Union Jack on the fin. (Nigel Jones)

91. Vulcan B.2(MRR) XH558 of No. 27 Sqn., from RAF Scampton, photographed at Goose Bay in August 1979. The aircraft is equipped with the upper-air sampling pods which were used in the squadron's secondary role. (Nigel Jones)

▼89

▲92   ▼93

94▲

92. XM648 was a Vulcan B.2 of No. 101 Sqn., RAF Waddington, and is seen here surrounded by Goose Bay's distinctive, brightly coloured ground-handling equipment, January 1980. Unlike in Europe, there was little threat of low-level surprise attack at Goose, and so base facilities and equipment were not camouflaged. (Nigel Jones)

93. Vulcan B.2 XM597 of No. 101 Sqn. about to touch down at RAF Waddington on 22 April 1982. The aircraft is almost certainly returning from a training sortie as part of the work-up to participation in the Falklands War: just a few days later, modified with a new paint scheme and equipped for wing-mounted pylons, '597 departed for Ascension Island, whence it took part in the historic anti-radar strikes using Shrike missiles. (Author)

94. Vulcan B.2 XM575, flown by Flt. Lt. Martin Withers DFC, approaching Runway 21 at RAF Waddington in late 1982. Several of the Vulcans in the background are ex-Falklands 'Black Buck' aircraft, with Dark Sea Grey undersides. Flt. Lt. Withers flew the first-ever war operation of the Vulcan when he piloted XM607 on the first 'Black Buck' strike against Port Stanley airfield during the Falklands War. (Mike Jenvey)

95. Personnel of No. 50 Sqn's line servicing unit retract the refuelling hose of K.2 tanker XH558 at Coningsby in June 1983. The hose was controlled by a remote-control box for servicing purposes. No. 50 Sqn. was operating from Coningsby while runway work was carried out at Waddington in preparation for the arrival of AEW Nimrods. (Author)

95▼

▲96 ▼97

96. Seen from the right-hand seat of a Vulcan K.2, a Victor K.2 tanker turns gently right during air-to-air refuelling operations in 1984. The refuelling areas over the North Sea and elsewhere require such operations to be conducted in turns, and lengthy transfers can involve flying a 'racetrack' pattern. Note the details of the Victor, especially the underwing positioning stripes, and the indicator lamps beside the hose aperture. (Mike Jenvey)

97. Vulcan B.2(MRR) XH563 is now in residence as the gate guardian at RAF Scampton, its erstwhile operational base when serving with No. 27 Sqn. This photograph was taken on the day on which the aircraft was moved into position; appropriately enough, the fin of the aircraft carries the badges of all four units which served with the Vulcan in its latter years at Scampton – No. 230 OCU and No. 617 Sqn. on the port side, and Nos. 27 and 35 Sqns. on the starboard side. Scampton's latest residents, the Red Arrows, overfly Scampton's last Vulcan. (Nigel Jones)

98. The majority of Vulcan B.1s carried serials beneath both wings, as shown here by XA901, photographed in June 1960 when in service with No. 230 OCU. Notice the squared-off wing tips with long probes and the small air scoop above the nosewheel doors, distinctive features of all B.1 Vulcans which were retained even after conversion to B.1A standard. (R. L. Ward)

99. A surprising number of Vulcans were allocated to development and trials work of great variety, one such being XA890, which spent a great deal of its service life shuttling to and from the A&AEE, the RAE and Woodford. The aircraft is seen here in 1963 when it was allocated to the RAE Radio Department. It is likely that the white-painted areas on the fin and wing leading edges are associated with the development work for which the aircraft was being used at this stage, the remainder of the airframe being natural metal except for the dielectric panels of the nose and fin cap.

▲100

100. XA894 was a Vulcan which spent all its service life as a test and development airframe. This aircraft was delivered to Filton in mid-1960 for installation of the Olympus 22R engine – which was to power the TSR.2 – in the bomb bay, in which configuration it first flew in February 1962. XA894 appeared at the 1962 SBAC show at Farnborough, where it is seen making a low-level pass. The aircraft was destroyed in December 1962 when an engine explosion during ground running caused a fuel tank fire. (R. L. Ward)

▼101

101. XA892 was another interesting Vulcan B.1 which spent the majority of its service career on trials work for the A&AEE and the RAE, returning to Woodford at the end of each successive period with these establishments. In June 1962 the aircraft was stripped to the bare minimum of equipment necessary for one final flight, from Farnborough to Halton, where it was allocated the code '16' and used for ground instructional training at No. 1 School of Technical Training. It was photographed in November 1962.

2, 103. There is little doubt that had the Skybolt programme
progressed to full operational use the subsequent history of the
Force, and probably that of the British aircraft industry, would
have been very different. The Douglas XAGM-87A Skybolt was to
be the first air-launched ballistic missile, and would have provided a
potent element of Britain's independent nuclear deterrent force,
whether in isolation or in conjunction with Polaris submarines. In the
event, the programme ran into difficulties and was cancelled, but not
before it had been established that the Vulcan B.2 was an ideal carrier
for a minimum of two missiles (and plans had been drawn up for a
version carrying up to six Skybolts). The major elements of the
system as applied to the Vulcan were wing-mounted pylons (hard-

points for which were included in production Vulcan B.2s in
anticipation of the missile) and controls at the Nav Plotter's position;
the installations seen here were for trials purposes, but it is unlikely
that service versions would have been very different. Note the steeply
raked rear edge of the pylon and its relationship to the wing leading
edge at the front, and the Avro badge. The control units provided
facilities for inputting and updating the navigational information
needed to enable the missile to find its way to the target once released,
in addition to the arming and releasing controls (one box for each
missile); the units were installed just above the Nav Plotter's Doppler
and navigation box. (British Aerospace)

▲104

104. XH537 at Woodford in 1962 carrying two dummy Skybolts for aerodynamic trials. No significant difficulties were encountered. (British Aerospace)

105. A side view of the dummy installation on XH537. Notice the long afterbody of the missile behind the fins, and the black and white fairing beneath the wing tip, probably housing cameras. The missile carries a standard RAF roundel and a Douglas Aircraft Corporation badge, the markings being in normal red/blue colours. Notice that the port sextant sight (next to the cockpit canopy) is extended. (British Aerospace)

106. A superb air-to-air shot of XH538 carrying live Skybolts, photographed on 12 July 1962. The aircraft is a fully equipped B.2 (XH537 lacked the wingtip dielectric panels associated with the aircraft's ECM systems), has an extra air intake mounted on the port bomb bay door, and has fairings, probably for cameras, beneath each wingtip and on the fuselage centreline immediately in front of the bomb bay. The port Skybolt has the same basic shape at the front as the dummy versions, but it has a more pointed nose, and carries the typical black and white markings associated with measuring equipment, whilst the missile on the starboard pylon has a simple conical nose and carries an RAF roundel. (British Aerospace)

107. XH537 in November 1962, getting airborne with two of the modified Skybolts which probably would have been the final version of the missile. Notice that there are photographic reference marks painted on the front sides of each pylon; the extreme tip of each missile is grey. Neither Skybolt trials Vulcan carried a refuelling probe, having what appear to be cameras fitted in its place. (British Aerospace)

▼105

▲108 ▼109

110▲   111▼

108. Part of the Vulcan B.2 production line in 1962, showing nose sections and (left) some assembly of wing leading edges. The nose sections are in various stages of completion, and each has a cockpit canopy stored nearby; work on most sections appears to be concentrated on fitting out the cockpits. The dinghy pack containers, located immediately behind the pilots' seats, are already in place. (British Aerospace)

109. Another part of the Vulcan B.2 line at Chadderton showing fuselage and inner wing/engine mounting sections being assembled. In most cases, the individual major sections of the aircraft were brought virtually to completion, with all wiring and plumbing installed, before being joined together to produce the finished machine. (British Aerospace)

110. Final assembly work at Chadderton. All the major assemblies have been put together, and final fitting out and skinning of joins are taking place. Engines are still to be installed, but the majority of the aircraft are substantially complete. (British Aerospace)

111. Three Olympus 200-Series engines are prominent in this view of the Final Assembly section at Chadderton. Views of aircraft without radomes are useful in emphasizing the pronounced droop of the top edge of the radome itself, and in showing to advantage the massive pressure bulkhead which forms the front of the cockpit. Note that the cockpit canopy is hinged at the rear edge, although this facility was intended for servicing purposes only. (British Aerospace)

55

▲112

112. XH558 was the first Vulcan B.2 to be delivered to No. 230 OCU, entering service on 1 July 1960. The aircraft is seen here on a pre-delivery flight, during the course of which the ram air turbine beneath the port air intakes was deployed. The RAT was installed for emergency use in the event of the engine-mounted alternators and the airborne auxiliary power pack failing, and could not be retracted in flight once extended. XH558 went on to enjoy a distinguished career with the RAF, being converted to B.2(MRR) standard and subsequently to a K.2 tanker; at the time of writing the aircraft is still in service, on the strength of the Vulcan Display Team. (British Aerospace)

113. XH538 was one of the more interesting Vulcan airframes. It is seen here very early in its career, a Vulcan B.2 in all respects except for the B.1 standard tailcone (and thus the absence of the Mk.2 ECM fit). The aircraft later served in both Blue Steel and Skybolt trials before being issued to the RAF as a standard B.2 bomber, finally ending its life with No. 35 Sqn. at RAF Scampton, whence it was

delivered to St. Athan for scrapping in March 1981. (British Aerospace)

114. XJ783, of No. 83 Sqn., RAF Scampton, seen at altitude; a standard B.2, it has yet to receive the distinctive antler badge of the squadron on its fin. Notice the dielectric panels on the upper surface of the fuselage (the circular one being the radio compass loop), the HF radio notch aerial in the fin root and the extensive chipping of the white paint finish along the lower intake lip. No nose probe is carried (British Aerospace)

115, 116. All-white Vulcans were by no means standardized when it came to sizes, styles and positions of markings. In photograph 115, XM575 of No. 617 Sqn., RAF Scampton, has the pale red triple lightning flashes of that unit on the fin but carries no squadron crest on the fuselage, whilst B.2 XL388 of No. 9 Sqn. (photograph 116) carries the fuselage crest but no fin badge. Neither aircraft is at this stage equipped with a nose probe.

▼113

114▲

115▲   116▼

▲117

117. XA903, the longest-lived Vulcan B.1, is seen here at Woodford during trials with development models of the Blue Steel stand-off bomb. These trials were related to the aerodynamic performance of the missile itself, and so no major modifications were made to the airframe of '903 to achieve a production-type fit between aircraft and missile. The colour of this development round has not been recorded, but it is likely to have been either dark blue or black. A camera fairing has been installed at the rear of the visual bombing blister. (British Aerospace)

118. XH537 was also used for Blue Steel trials; here the aircraft is at altitude with the Blue Steel ventral fin extended. Notice that the missile body and fins have black lines for photographic purposes and that the aircraft has a camera fairing built in to the rear of the visual bombing blister. (British Aerospace)

119. All Blue Steel Vulcans had 200-Series Olympus engines with the longer, 'toed-out' jetpipes and were designated B.2A. Here XL445 is at altitude. The aircraft is from No. 27 Sqn. and features that unit's large-size elephant badge in green on the fin. (British Aerospace)

120. XL320 of the Scampton Wing at altitude and carrying a Blue Steel. The aircraft exhibits a distinctly worn uppersurface camouflage scheme – notice the repainted areas on the wing leading edge and around the air intake. The black coating of the nose radome is also heavily weathered. (British Aerospace)

121. XL446, also of the Scampton Wing, demonstrates the usual amount of underwing staining for a Vulcan B.2, in this case coming particularly from the alternator cooling ducts beneath each engine. Note that this aircraft has ECM aerial plates between both sets of engines; the flat part of these aerials was rarely painted. (British Aerospace)

▼118

▼119

▲122 ▼123

122. A superb view of the underside of a Waddington Wing Vulcan
.1A in about 1966. The bomb bay was identical in size to that of the
.2, as was the ECM fit. All the elements of the latter can be
identified here, including the three dome aerials on the flat plate
etween the starboard engines, the wing-tip dielectric panels, and the
nlarged rear tailcone housing the transmitters/receivers. Notice the
bsence of underwing roundels and serials. (No. 50 Sqn. via Ray
each)

123. Vulcan B.1A XA910 of the Waddington Wing, seen at RAF
Muharraq in 1966 while on the eastabout reinforcement route to the
Far East. Overseas deployments of this nature were normal for
Vulcans serving in the conventional-bombing role, although no
modifications to camouflage were carried out during them. The
deployments, as well as achieving political objectives, provided
valuable training in navigation skills *en route*. (A. J. Mayhew)

124▲

124. The Operations Room at RAF Honington in July 1963. The
board on the left of the photograph gives availability and tasking
details of all Honington-based aircraft, while that along the side of the
room is for overseas movements, and includes space for stopovers
and flight stages. The communications equipment in the centre of the
room would provide secure links with HQ Bomber Command and
direct to the squadrons; on Quick Reaction Alert (QRA) duties the
Ops Room would also be able to speak directly with the crews of the
aircraft waiting at readiness. (Wg. Cdr. Bryn Lewis)

125. XJ783 being refuelled on its dispersal at RAF Waddington in
January 1966; at this time all RAF ground equipment was still
painted blue, or yellow for certain items. The tanker is linked up to
the refuelling connections in the port main wheel bay. The aircraft is
finished in high-gloss camouflage, with distinct 'feathering'
between the colours, and has white undersides. (Crown Copyright)

125▼

▲126   ▼127

128▲

126–129. In July 1966 a Waddington Wing Vulcan B.1A, XA912, made what is probably the only visit ever by a Vulcan to Sharjah. The flight was made to determine whether the Bahrain base was suitable for the aircraft since the changeover from Canberras to Vulcans at Cyprus was imminent, and Sharjah had been used by the Cyprus-based Canberras as an armament practice location. Conditions at Sharjah were not ideal even for Canberras; it had a short and very narrow runway, and this, combined with the problems of high temperatures, made it very difficult for a heavily loaded Canberra to get airborne much after 0900hrs. in summer. XA912 came and went in the early morning with just enough fuel for the flight to and from Bahrain, and the trial was never repeated.

130. (Next spread) A dramatic night-time photograph of Vulcan B.1A XH483 of the Waddington Wing, about 1965. Note that the bomb bay doors are open and that the external ground power source is connected. All V-bomber permanent bases had provision for reasonable illumination of the aircraft from the outside, in addition to the servicing lights built in to the aircraft themselves, and servicing normally took place round the clock throughout the long years of QRA. (Crown Copyright)

129▼

▲131 ▼132

. Vulcan B.2 XM649, photo-
[grap]hed at low level in the early
[197]0s. The upper surface
[cam]ouflage scheme applied to
[Vul]cans from 1964 is here shown
[to a]dvantage; the pattern
[rem]ained broadly similar
[thr]oughout the service life of the
[Vu]lcan, although the standards
[of f]inish changed from gloss to
[mat]t over twenty-plus years.
[On]ly one roundel, on the port
[upp]er surface, was applied to
[Vu]lcans in the early years of
[cam]ouflage, and the photograph
[als]o shows the extent to which
[the] camouflage colours extended
[int]o the air intakes. (British
[Ae]rospace)

[13]2. Vulcan B.2s of the Near
[Eas]t Air Force (NEAF) Bomber
[Win]g (Nos. 9 and 35 Sqns.) at
[RA]F Akrotiri, Cyprus, in 1969,
[the] year in which the Wing was
[for]med. The establishment of
[thi]s Wing was the result of the
[nee]d to provide a contribution to
[NA]TO force levels in the area,
[an]d also of the need to support
[the] Central Treaty Organization
[(C]ENTO), which had no
[str]ucture or forces of its own. A
[str]ong presence in the area was
[par]ticularly important to
[cou]nter Soviet influence,
[esp]ecially once the last RAF
[bas]e in Africa (El Adem, Libya)
[clo]sed early in 1970. Strangely,
[thr]oughout the six years of the
[NE]AF Wing, neither
[squ]adron's aircraft had any
[ch]ange in their basic camouflage
[sc]heme, presumably because of
[the] very wide range of tasks
[wh]ich they might be called upon
[to] carry out operationally, and
[be]cause their main task in a time
[of] major crisis would have been
[ag]ainst targets in the Soviet
[U]nion. (Crown Copyright via
[Gp]. Capt. M. J. Milligan)

[13]3, 134. Two photographs
[sh]owing bomb handling at RAF
[W]addington. In illustration 133
[th]e upper four bombs, in this
[ca]se Mk. 15 1,000lb weapons,
[h]ave been attached to the frame,
[an]d the lower three are being
[p]icked up. The airman on the
[ri]ght is controlling the crane,
[w]hile the airman on the left is
[h]olding a local release
[c]ontroller, used to attach the
[b]ombs to the frame. In photo-
[g]raph 134 a loaded bomb frame
[i]s being installed into the bay of a
[V]ulcan. Note the two hydraulic
[j]acks for this purpose on each
[s]ide of the frame – bombing-up
[w]as achieved without the use of
[e]xternal equipment other than
[t]he bomb trolley itself. The air-
[c]raft has a bomb bay fuel tank
[i]nstalled in the forward position.
[(]Crown Copyright via
[P]. McGrath)